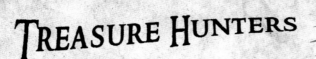

TREASURE HUNTERS

LOST CITIES

NICOLA BARBER

Chicago, Illinois

© 2013 Raintree
an imprint of Capstone Global Library, LLC
Chicago, Illinois

Edited by Laura Knowles, Adam Miller,
Harriet Milles, and Helen Cox Cannons
Designed by Victoria Allen
Original illustrations © Capstone Global Library
Ltd 2013
Illustrated by Martin Bustamante
Picture research by Tracy Cummins

Originated by Capstone Global Library Ltd.
Production by Alison Parsons
Printed and bound in China by Leo Paper
Products Ltd

16 15 14 13 12
10 9 8 7 6 5 4 3 2 1

**Library of Congress Cataloging-in-Publication
Data**
Barber, Nicola.
Lost cities / Nicola Barber.
    p. cm.—(Treasure hunters)
Includes bibliographical references and index.
ISBN 978-1-4109-4952-3 (hb)—ISBN 978-1-4109-
4959-2 (pb) 1. Extinct cities—Juvenile literature.
2. Archaeology—History—Juvenile literature.
3. Civilization, Ancient—Juvenile literature. 4.
Legends—Juvenile literature. I. Title.
    CC176.B36 2013
    930.1—dc23   2012012891

Acknowledgments
We would like to thank the following for
permission to reproduce photographs:
Alamy pp.4 (©Robert Harding Picture Library
Ltd), 33 bot (©Imagestate Media Partners
Limited - Impact Photos); Art Resource pp.16
(Gianni Dagli Orti/The Art Archive, 34 (Dietrich
Gra/Ethnologisches Museum, Staatliche Museen,
Berlin, Germany); Corbis pp.5 (©Ira Block/National
Geographic Society), 14 top (©George Steinmetz),
15 (©K.M. Westermann), 17 (©Bettmann), 21
(©Hulton-Deutsch Collection), 28 bot (©Mimmo
Jodice), 29 & 31 (©Roger Ressmeyer), 36 (©Arne
Hodalic); Getty Images pp.13 (©John Mitchell),
22 (©Time & Life Pictures/Getty Images), 25
(©Alberto Incrocc; NASA p. 12 top; National
Geographic p.39 (©BINGHAM, HIRAM - YALE
PEABODY MUSEUM); Newscom pp.9 (©Donald
Nausbaum/Robert Harding), 18 (akg-images/
Peter Connolly), 20, 23, 35 (©akg-images), 37 bot
(©AFP PHOTO/AFP/Getty Images); Photoshot
p.10 (©UPPA); Reuters p.41(©Pilar Olivares);
Shutterstock pp.1 (©Pani), 6 (©Lukasz Kurbiel), 7
(©Connors Bros.), 8-9 (©apdesign), 11 (©Rechitan
Sorin), 12 bot (©Mechanik), 14 bot (©Iwona
Grodzka), 19 (©Eky Studio), 24 (©Catmando), 28
top (©Warren Goldswain), 30 (©Alfio Ferlito), 31
bot (©Joy Fera), 31 mid (©Jelena Voronova), 32
(©kated), 33 t.l. (©J. Helgason), 33 t.r. (©Scisetti
Alfio), 37 top (©Galyna Andrushko), 38 (©Arvind
Balaraman), 40 (©Steve Estvanik), 42 (©Patrick
Poendl), 43 (©Linda Bucklin). Design features:
©Shutterstock.

Cover photo of Angkor Wat, Ta Prohm temple,
Cambodia, Shutterstock (©davidk).

Expert consultant
We would like to thank Dr. Mark
Horton for his invaluable help
in the preparation of this book.
Dr. Horton is a professor of
archaeology at the University of
Bristol, England, and a specialist
in the archaeology of historical
societies around the world.

Guided Reading Level: W

CONTENTS

LOOKING FOR LOST CITIES

How do cities get lost? It is a good question! Think of one of the world's many modern-day cities, such as Los Angeles, London, or Tokyo, and it is difficult to imagine how they could ever be "lost." Ancient cities were, of course, many times smaller than our modern-day mega-cities. And over the centuries, many of them have been abandoned and forgotten.

Mohenjo-Daro, in modern-day Pakistan, was one of the world's earliest cities. It was abandoned in around 1800 BCE.

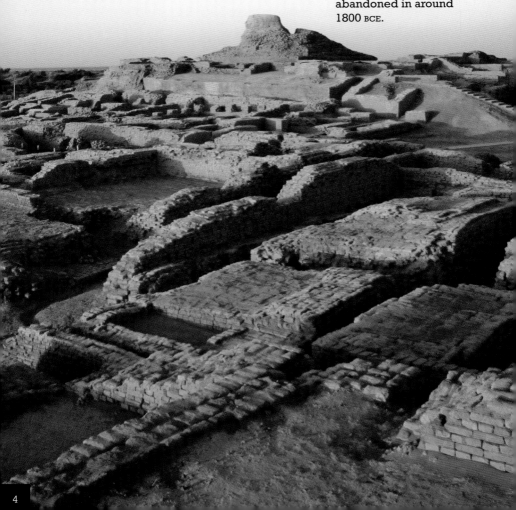

WHAT HAPPENED?

There are many reasons why a city can become lost. In some cases, a natural disaster such as an earthquake, a volcanic eruption, or flooding can simply overwhelm a city. This is what happened to Pompeii, in Italy, when the volcano Vesuvius erupted violently. You can find out more about the swift and terrifying destruction of Pompeii on pages 24 to 33.

Other cities were abandoned by their inhabitants because of war. In some places, the food or water supply seems to have been disrupted, forcing a city's residents to move elsewhere. But sometimes we just do not know why a place that had once been bustling and busy was deserted by the people who lived there.

In 1250 CE, on the floodplain of the Mississippi River (in present-day Illinois), there stood one of the biggest cities in the world. At that time, the city of Cahokia covered nearly 6 square miles (15 square kilometers) and was home to up to 20,000 people—as big as London or Paris at the time. Yet by 1400, it had been abandoned. Today, the only reminders of this city are more than 100 earth mounds (see the photo below).

LOST... AND FOUND

Most "lost" cities are not absolutely lost. Local people often know something about the mysterious ruins that lie deep in a jungle or are covered by desert sands. But it is only when an outsider comes along to investigate that people realize what these ruins really are.

This is what happened to the American historian and explorer Hiram Bingham, high in the Andes Mountains in 1911. Bingham was looking for the lost cities of the Inca people. He was amazed when a local guide led him to some spectacular ruins, high on a mountaintop. Although Bingham was not the first to find the ruins, he was the first person to bring them to the attention of the wider world. You can find out more about Bingham's "discovery" on pages 34 to 41.

Machu Picchu is in the Andes Mountains.

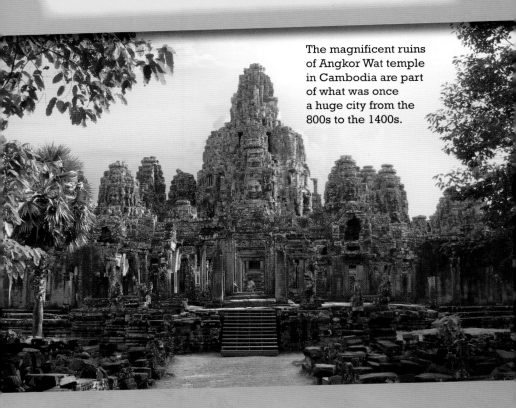

The magnificent ruins of Angkor Wat temple in Cambodia are part of what was once a huge city from the 800s to the 1400s.

WHY LOOK?

Why do people look for lost cities? Historians and archaeologists want to know more about the people who once lived there: what they ate, who they worshipped, and what jobs they did. And there is always the chance that something really unusual may turn up, including treasure like gold or silver!

UBAR: CITY IN THE SANDS

Sand, sand, and more sand … The Rub al-Khali (Arabic for the "Empty Quarter") is the largest area of uninterrupted sand in the world. It covers much of the southern Arabian Peninsula, with wind-blown dunes rising almost 1,000 feet (300 meters) high. It is fiercely hot, very dry, and virtually uninhabited.

FRANKINCENSE

Frankincense is a resin, similar to gum, that comes from the trunks of the Boswellia trees that grow in southern Arabia. Since ancient times, it has been highly prized for its delicious smell when it is burned and for its use in medicines.

THE ANCIENT PEOPLE OF 'AD

Tales of a fabulous city that had long-since disappeared beneath the sands of the Rub al-Khali have been passed down for centuries. References to such a city appear in the holy book of Islam, the Qur'an. The nomadic people of the deserts, the Bedouin, also have many stories about an ancient trading city inhabited by the people of 'Ad.

According to these tales, the city was famed for its trade in frankincense, but its people became arrogant and were punished when the city suffered a terrible calamity and was destroyed.

"NOW THE 'AD BEHAVED ARROGANTLY THROUGH THE LAND, AGAINST (ALL) TRUTH AND REASON, AND SAID: 'WHO IS SUPERIOR TO US IN STRENGTH?'"

HOW THE PEOPLE OF 'AD ARE DESCRIBED IN THE QUR'AN

DANGEROUS LANDS

The tales of the lost city in the sands fascinated explorers. But a trip into the Rub al-Khali was not to be undertaken lightly. The desert covers an area about the size of Texas and has extremes of temperature ranging from over 122 degrees Fahrenheit (50 degrees Celsius) during the day to below freezing at night. With few sources of water, this wasn't a good place to get lost.

Harry St. John Philby was a fluent Arabic speaker and wore Bedouin clothes. In 1932, he crossed the Rub al-Khali of Arabia.

RACE ACROSS THE SANDS

In 1931, a British explorer named Bertram Thomas became the first European to make the journey across the Rub al-Khali. In doing so, he beat his fellow-explorer and friend, Harry St. John Philby, who had hoped and planned to be the first to cross the desert sands.

Once Philby had recovered from his disappointment, he resolved to go anyway. In fact, Philby wanted to do more than just cross the Rub al-Khali. He wanted to look for the city the Bedouins had told him about—a city called Ubar.

Philby started his journey across the "ocean of sand" that is the Rub al-Khali with 32 camels and 15 Bedouin men.

Spotted from space

It was modern technology that allowed archaeologists finally to locate the long-lost city of Ubar. Images taken from space can show up marks on Earth's surface that cannot be seen from the ground. In the Rub al-Khali, pictures taken by the *Challenger* space shuttle revealed ancient tracks created thousands of years ago by camel caravans. And it seemed that many of these tracks led to Ubar.

FOLLOWING CLUES

Philby did not find Ubar, and neither did several later expeditions. But the pictures taken from the space shuttle, and others from satellites, gave explorers and archaeologists some important clues.

In the 1990s, an expedition that included American filmmaker Nicholas Clapp, British explorer Ranulph Fiennes, and American archaeologist Juris Zarins set out into the Rub al-Khali.

These images of the Rub al-Khali were both taken by satellites. The site of Ubar is too small to show up, but tracks leading to the site helped archaeologists figure out where it was.

RUINS ARE FOUND!

Even with all the information from the space images, it still took a great deal of painstaking and patient work before Clapp's expedition finally found what it had been looking for. At a watering hole called Shis'r, there was an old Arab fort. But beneath and around the fort lay older ruins. Were these the remains of Ubar?

DANGER: SNAKES!

If you ever find yourself on an archaeological dig in the desert, remember to keep an eye out for snakes! Hiding under the boxes in the supply tent, the expedition found an unremarkable-looking small brown snake. It turned out to be a deadly carpet viper—very poisonous and very bad-tempered! Luckily, no one was bitten.

EXCAVATIONS

The excavations at Shis'r uncovered a small settlement with a fort, walls, and watchtowers. The people of this ancient city drew water from a well fed by water in a cave, deep underground. This water was essential for the inhabitants—it was the only water for hundreds of miles. Traveling camel caravans also stopped there to replenish their supplies. But excavations quickly revealed that the source of the water also brought about the city's downfall around 800 years ago.

THE SINKHOLE

The legends of Ubar told how the city had come to a terrible end when it sank into the sands of the desert. The truth behind the legend appeared to lie in the large sinkhole at Shis'r. A sinkhole is a hole in the ground formed when the roof of an underground cave collapses below. When the cave beneath the well collapsed at Shis'r, it took much of the city with it. Did this prove that the city was indeed Ubar?

In this aerial view, you can see the modern settlement at Shis'r beyond the hole that swallowed up the ancient city.

WAS THIS UBAR?

From around 3200 BCE until its sudden collapse in around 300 CE, the ancient settlement at Shis'r was a thriving place on the route of the frankincense trade. Camel caravans stopped at the city to fill up with water and supplies before setting off across the Rub al-Khali, loaded with valuable frankincense.

Today, experts around the world still disagree about whether this was the fabled city of Ubar or not. Many now believe that Ubar was the name of a region rather than a city. But they do agree that the excavations at Shis'r were of great importance for our understanding of life in ancient Arabia.

These are what some people believe are the ruins of the city of Ubar.

WHAT DID THEY FIND?

The archaeologists working at the Shis'r site did not find any gold or treasure. But they did find pieces of pottery from far-off lands— Persia, Rome, and Greece. These suggest that the city was indeed once a busy trading center. The sturdy city walls and watchtowers were probably built to defend the precious supply of water from raiding Bedouin tribes.

THE SEARCH FOR TROY

Imagine starting work on an archaeological excavation to find
a long-lost city, and then digging up not just one city—but nine!
This is exactly what happened to the German businessman
and archaeologist Heinrich Schliemann.

Ever since he was a small boy, Schliemann had been fascinated
by the legendary city of Troy. At that time, no one knew whether
Troy was a real place, or whether it was just a make-believe city
in stories and poems. Schliemann was determined to find out.

STORIES OF TROY

As a child, Schliemann's favorite story came from the *Iliad*, an epic poem written by the ancient Greek poet Homer. In the *Iliad*, Homer recounts the events of a few weeks in the long-running war between the Greeks and the people of Troy—the Trojans. During this war, the city of Troy was besieged by the Greeks for 10 long years. The war finally ended with the destruction of the city.

HEINRICH SCHLIEMANN

Born: 1822

Died: 1890

- *According to Schliemann, as a boy of seven years old, he vowed to find the true location of the real Troy.*

- *One of Schliemann's first jobs was as a cabin boy on a ship that was wrecked during a storm off the coast of Holland.*

- *Schliemann taught himself many languages, including English, Dutch, Russian, French, Spanish, Portuguese, and Italian.*

- *Schliemann made a fortune working in Russia trading indigo dye and also during the Gold Rush in California.*

THE SEARCH BEGINS

In 1863, Schliemann decided to retire from business. He was so wealthy that he had enough money to devote the rest of his life to his great obsession—the search for Troy. Using clues from Homer's *Iliad*, Schliemann traveled to Turkey to begin the search for likely sites.

Schliemann was not alone in his quest. Another amateur archaeologist, a British man named Frank Calvert, had done some excavations at a mound in a remote spot called Hisarlik in western Turkey. Calvert convinced Schliemann that Hisarlik could be the site of ancient Troy.

Is this what the ancient city of Troy once looked like?

WHICH CITY?

Schliemann began excavating at Hisarlik in 1871. With teams of local workers, he sunk deep shafts down into the mound. It soon became apparent that there was a whole series of ancient cities buried beneath the mound, one on top of another. Clearly, Troy had been destroyed and rebuilt many times. But which one was Homer's Troy?

In his determination to get down to the bottom—and oldest—layer, Schliemann ordered his workers to move huge amounts of stone and rubble. But when Schliemann examined the ruins at the bottom of the trenches, he decided they were too old to be those of Homer's Troy.

Working back up, he came across layers of ash that suggested evidence of fire. In the *Iliad*, Homer describes how Troy was burned to the ground by the Greeks. Schliemann decided that this was the layer of remains he needed to excavate. Unfortunately, the earlier digging had destroyed a large area of the city that Schliemann now believed was Troy.

Uncovering Treasure

In 1873, the workers at Hisarlik uncovered a town wall and a big gate. These were important finds, but Schliemann was on the lookout for something even more exciting. According to Homer, Priam was the ruler of Troy during the war with the Greeks. Schliemann firmly believed that as the siege of the city dragged on, Priam must have found somewhere to hide his most precious belongings.

In May 1873, something happened to convince him that he was right. While clearing rubble away from a wall, Schliemann caught sight of the glint of metal. He immediately sent his workmen for a lunch break, so that he could examine his find secretly.

Schliemann's excavations at Troy revealed walls and a big gate.

"WHILE THE MEN WERE RESTING AND EATING, I CUT OUT THE TREASURE WITH A LARGE KNIFE. THIS ... INVOLVED GREAT RISK, SINCE THE WALL OF THE FORTIFICATION BENEATH WHICH I HAD TO DIG THREATENED EVERY MOMENT TO FALL ON ME. BUT THE SIGHT OF SO MANY OBJECTS, EVERY ONE OF WHICH IS OF INESTIMABLE VALUE TO ARCHAEOLOGY, MADE ME RECKLESS. I NEVER THOUGHT OF ANY DANGER."

SCHLIEMANN DESCRIBING HIS DISCOVERY OF
"PRIAM'S TREASURE"

PRIAM'S TREASURE

The so-called "Priam's treasure" (shown here) included a copper shield, a beautiful silver vase, many gold and copper plates and cups, and fine golden jewelry. In fact, we now know that this treasure had nothing to do with Priam, but rather came from a layer over 1,000 years older than "Homeric" Troy.

SMUGGLING AND LIES

According to the account written by Schliemann, he removed the treasure from the ground and handed it to his wife, Sophia, who wrapped the precious objects in her scarf. Under the terms agreed upon for the excavation, Schliemann was supposed to share any treasure found at the site half-and-half with the Turkish authorities. To avoid this, Schliemann smuggled the treasure out of Turkey and hid it in Greece.

In 1874, Schliemann published a book about his findings at Hisarlik, and his wife, Sophia, appeared in public wearing the jewelry found at Troy. The Turkish authorities were furious when they realized what Schliemann had done. In the end, Schliemann traded some of the treasure with the Turkish government and paid a large fine. Only then was he allowed to go back to Hisarlik to continue the excavations.

In this photo, Schliemann's wife, Sophia, wears some of the jewelry found at the excavation of Troy.

The treasure kept by Schliemann never went back to Turkey. It ended up in the Royal Museums of Berlin, in Germany. During World War II (1939–1945), it was carefully packed away and hidden in a bunker beneath the Berlin Zoo. But in the last days of the war, Soviet troops found it, and it was stolen once again. It disappeared completely until 1993, when it was put on display in Moscow, in Russia. Despite some negotiations for its return, it is still there.

TROY TODAY

The excavations that continue at Hisarlik today are much more organized and scientific than Schliemann's! Archaeologists now believe that the mound contains the remains of 10 settlements, spanning 4,500 years of occupation. Troy was built at the crossing point between Europe and Asia, which made it a target throughout its history. This explains why it was such a well-defended fortress.

POMPEII: BURIED ALIVE

IT IS THE MORNING OF AUGUST 24, 79 CE. IN THE ROMAN CITY OF POMPEII, IN SOUTHERN ITALY, THERE IS A SENSE OF UNEASE IN THE AIR. THERE HAVE BEEN A FEW EARTH TREMORS OVER THE PAST FEW DAYS. FOR MANY IN THE CITY, THESE SMALL TREMORS BRING BACK MEMORIES OF A BIG EARTHQUAKE THAT DEVASTATED PARTS OF THE CITY 17 YEARS AGO, IN 62 CE. IS THERE ANOTHER EARTHQUAKE ON THE WAY?

VESUVIUS

For any townspeople in Pompeii who looked toward the top of the mountain that lay close to the city, the sense of unease may have gotten worse. A red glow in the sky showed that this was no ordinary mountain. It was a volcano—and it was active. But Mount Vesuvius had not erupted for nearly 300 years, and no one in Pompeii had any reason to believe it was about to do so. When Vesuvius blew its top, the people of Pompeii were completely unprepared.

The ancient Romans did not know, as we do today, that earth tremors can be a sign that a volcano is about to erupt.

This is the crater of Mount Vesuvius today.

PLINY'S LETTER

We know about the eruption from an eyewitness account in a letter (at right) written by a Roman lawyer, Pliny the Younger. Pliny was staying in a nearby town and was close enough to see the eruption.

"ASHES WERE ALREADY FALLING, NOT AS YET VERY THICKLY. I LOOKED AROUND: A DENSE BLACK CLOUD WAS COMING UP BEHIND US, SPREADING OVER THE EARTH LIKE A FLOOD ... WE HAD SCARCELY SAT DOWN TO REST WHEN DARKNESS FELL, NOT THE DARK OF A MOONLESS OR CLOUDY NIGHT, BUT AS IF THE LAMP HAD BEEN PUT OUT IN A CLOSED ROOM."

Pompeii's last day

1 Mount Vesuvius begins to erupt on the morning of August 24, 79 CE.

3 Many townspeople flee the city. Those who stay face certain death.

4 Around midnight, a deadly pyroclastic flow of hot ash, rocks, and gas flows down the sides of the volcano at a speed of around 62 miles (100 kilometers) per hour.

2 Ash and volcanic rocks fall onto the streets of Pompeii.

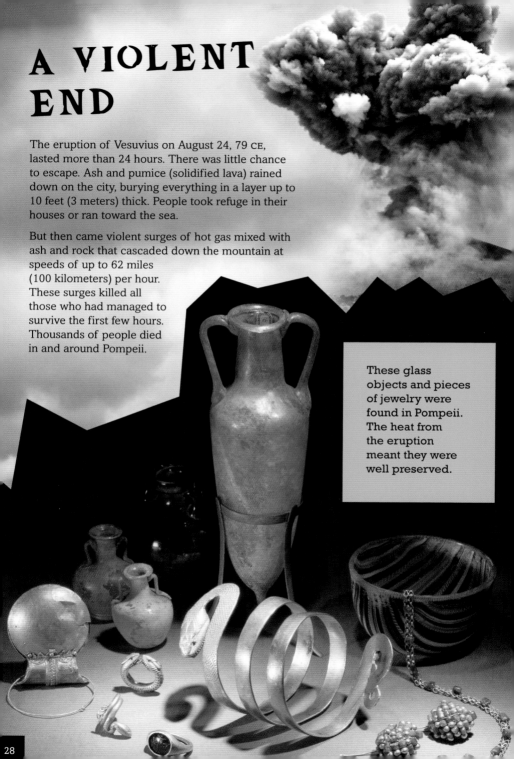

A VIOLENT END

The eruption of Vesuvius on August 24, 79 CE, lasted more than 24 hours. There was little chance to escape. Ash and pumice (solidified lava) rained down on the city, burying everything in a layer up to 10 feet (3 meters) thick. People took refuge in their houses or ran toward the sea.

But then came violent surges of hot gas mixed with ash and rock that cascaded down the mountain at speeds of up to 62 miles (100 kilometers) per hour. These surges killed all those who had managed to survive the first few hours. Thousands of people died in and around Pompeii.

These glass objects and pieces of jewelry were found in Pompeii. The heat from the eruption meant they were well preserved.

BURIED AND FORGOTTEN

The disaster was so catastrophic that the Romans made no attempt to rebuild the city. It lay buried beneath a thick layer of ash and mud for more than 1,000 years. The name of Pompeii was forgotten.

In the 1700s, workmen digging in the area uncovered some of the remains, and soon there was great interest in the buried city. When a stone bearing the inscription *Rei publicae Pompeianorum* ("Commonwealth of Pompeians") was uncovered in 1763, the city even got its name back.

Today, the ruins of Pompeii are uncovered once again. You can see Mount Vesuvius in the background.

Fishy evidence

Evidence for the date when Vesuvius erupted comes from written sources such as Pliny the Younger's letters. But this evidence has recently been confirmed by a more unusual investigation. Scientists have analyzed traces of fish sauce (see page 33) found in jars in Pompeii. Based on the type of fish used to make the sauce and the state of the sauce, they are sure that the eruption happened around the end of August in 79 CE.

PLUNDERING POMPEII

The first people to excavate Pompeii were interested only in the treasures—the wall paintings, statues, and jewelry—that could be removed. They were willing to smash down walls and to remove paintings and mosaics to get what they wanted.

It was an Italian archaeologist, Giuseppe Fiorelli, who finally put a stop to the plunder. When Fiorelli took over in 1860, he divided the city into nine sections and organized methodical excavations, layer by layer. He made careful notes of where things were found.

GIUSEPPE FIORELLI

Born: 1823

Died: 1896

· He first worked at Pompeii in the 1840s, but in 1848 was imprisoned by the king of Naples because of his political (and archaeological) views.

· He founded a school of archaeology and pioneered many of the techniques still used in archaeology today.

· The technique of making plaster casts, invented by Fiorelli, is today known as the Fiorelli process.

This is one of the mosaics found in Pompeii.

Plaster casts

Fiorelli invented a way to preserve the shapes of the bodies of the people who had died in the city. After the eruption, the volcanic ash had set and hardened around the victims' bodies. Over time, the bodies had decayed away to nothing, leaving hollows in the ash. Fiorelli realized that these hollows were like molds. If he filled the molds with plaster, he would recreate the exact shapes of the victims' bodies. The results were amazingly and uncomfortably lifelike (see above)!

FROZEN IN TIME

The uncovering of Pompeii revealed an ancient Roman city, frozen in time. What makes Pompeii so special for archaeologists and ancient historians today is that this was an ordinary city, with people going about their ordinary business. We have learned huge amounts about everyday life in Roman times from the excavations at Pompeii.

WORK AND PLAY

Pompeii was a bustling and thriving city in 79 CE. There were markets, stores, workshops, inns, and a flourishing wool industry. The people of Pompeii also enjoyed their leisure time at the baths, at the theater, and at the games.

CAVE CANEM! (BEWARE OF THE DOG!)

Visitors to one of the houses uncovered in Pompeii were greeted with this warning, spelled out in a mosaic on the floor. Above it was a fierce black mosaic dog, promising trouble for anyone who threatened the inhabitants of this house!

FOOD

What did people eat in Pompeii? When Vesuvius erupted, there was bread baking in the ovens at the city's many bakeries. In some cases, the volcanic ash from the eruption sealed the ovens, preserving the loaves of bread inside. It is extremely unusual for items of food to survive over the centuries.

The incredible heat of the eruption preserved not only the loaves of bread, but also eggs, walnuts, almonds, dates, figs, and olives. A popular speciality was a smelly fish sauce called garum, which the Pompeiians used a bit like ketchup. It was a sauce to go with everything!

This ancient Roman bread was preserved in the bakers' ovens at Pompeii by the eruption of Vesuvius.

PANI

LOST CITIES OF THE INCAS

For nearly 100 years, the Incas ruled over an expanding empire that eventually stretched about 2,250 miles (3,620 kilometers) down the western coast of South America. The Inca's capital was Cuzco, a city high in the Andes Mountains.

When Spanish *conquistadors* (conquerors) began to explore Inca territory in the 1520s, it soon became clear to them that this was a wealthy land, with possibilities for great riches and treasure …

Emperor Atahualpa

TAKING ADVANTAGE

In 1532, a small force of Spanish *conquistadors* under the command of Francisco Pizarro returned to the land of the Incas. They found the empire in turmoil. An outbreak of smallpox had killed many thousands of people, and a bitter civil war had just come to an end. The Spanish were quick to take advantage of the weak state of the empire. They captured the Inca emperor, Atahualpa, and held him hostage.

THE RANSOM

As the price for his freedom, Atahualpa offered the Spanish *conquistadors* enough gold to fill the room he was imprisoned in, as well as silver to fill two more rooms. The Incas delivered the ransom—but the *conquistadors* killed Atahualpa anyway.

The Inca Empire was a land of great riches. At Potosi, high in the Andes, the Spanish found a mountain that was seemingly made of silver. They established a mining town there in 1546, which quickly became one of the wealthiest towns in the world. From Potosi, thousands of tons of silver were transported to the coast and across the Atlantic Ocean to Spain.

INCA DEFIANCE

The Spanish *conquistadors* chose a new Inca leader, Manco Inca, to act as emperor under their direction. But Manco Inca defied the Spanish and retreated first to the wild Vitcos valley, and then to a stronghold in the remote mountainous region of Vilcabamba.

The Incas continued to mount raids against the Spanish until 1572, when the last Inca ruler was captured and executed. Vitcos and Vilcabamba were destroyed by the Spanish and left to disappear into the jungle.

LOST CITIES AND TREASURE

Ever since the fall of the Incas, there have been legends of lost Inca cities and hidden Inca treasure. Many stories tell how wealthy Incas, fleeing from the Spanish invaders, hid huge treasure troves of gold, silver, and precious stones.

Documents written by Spanish explorers in the 1500s and 1600s describe Inca cities rich in gold, silver, and gemstones. Such tales attracted many treasure hunters, explorers, and archaeologists to go looking for Inca sites in the 20th century. One of these was Hiram Bingham.

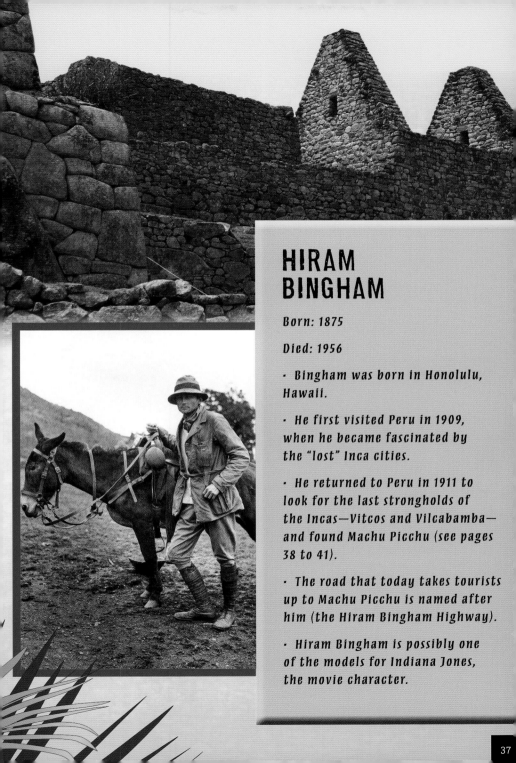

HIRAM BINGHAM

Born: 1875

Died: 1956

· Bingham was born in Honolulu, Hawaii.

· He first visited Peru in 1909, when he became fascinated by the "lost" Inca cities.

· He returned to Peru in 1911 to look for the last strongholds of the Incas—Vitcos and Vilcabamba— and found Machu Picchu (see pages 38 to 41).

· The road that today takes tourists up to Machu Picchu is named after him (the Hiram Bingham Highway).

· Hiram Bingham is possibly one of the models for Indiana Jones, the movie character.

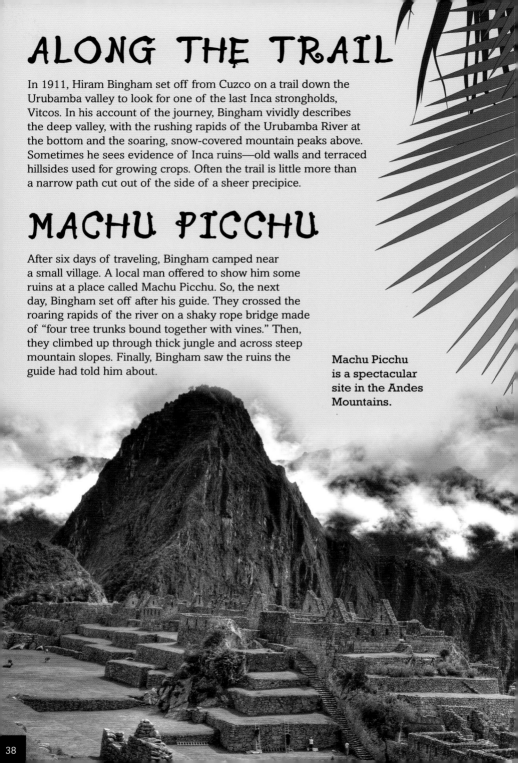

ALONG THE TRAIL

In 1911, Hiram Bingham set off from Cuzco on a trail down the Urubamba valley to look for one of the last Inca strongholds, Vitcos. In his account of the journey, Bingham vividly describes the deep valley, with the rushing rapids of the Urubamba River at the bottom and the soaring, snow-covered mountain peaks above. Sometimes he sees evidence of Inca ruins—old walls and terraced hillsides used for growing crops. Often the trail is little more than a narrow path cut out of the side of a sheer precipice.

MACHU PICCHU

After six days of traveling, Bingham camped near a small village. A local man offered to show him some ruins at a place called Machu Picchu. So, the next day, Bingham set off after his guide. They crossed the roaring rapids of the river on a shaky rope bridge made of "four tree trunks bound together with vines." Then, they climbed up through thick jungle and across steep mountain slopes. Finally, Bingham saw the ruins the guide had told him about.

Machu Picchu is a spectacular site in the Andes Mountains.

"...WE COULD MAKE OUT A MAZE OF ANCIENT WALLS, THE RUINS OF BUILDINGS MADE OF BLOCKS OF GRANITE, SOME OF WHICH WERE BEAUTIFULLY FITTED TOGETHER IN THE MOST REFINED STYLE OF INCA ARCHITECTURE ... THE SUPERIOR CHARACTER OF THE STONE WORK ... LED ME TO BELIEVE THAT MACHU PICCHU MIGHT PROVE TO BE THE LARGEST AND MOST IMPORTANT RUIN DISCOVERED IN SOUTH AMERICA SINCE THE DAYS OF THE SPANISH CONQUEST."

HIRAM BINGHAM'S DESCRIPTION OF MACHU PICCHU IN *NATIONAL GEOGRAPHIC* MAGAZINE, 1913

WORLDWIDE FAME

The Spanish *conquistadors* never found Machu Picchu, but it was well known to local people, and it is likely that other outsiders had visited it before Bingham. Bingham returned to Peru in 1912 and 1915, and he wrote many magazine articles and books about Machu Picchu. Around the world, people were amazed and fascinated by this beautiful Inca ruin.

WHAT WAS IT?

What do we know about Machu Picchu? Most archaeologists believe that it was built as a kind of country estate for the Inca emperor Pachacuti, who ruled from 1438 to 1471, at the height of the Inca Empire. Others believe that it was a place for religious worship.

The Incas constructed stone walls and buildings without using mortar to hold the stones together. They cut the blocks of stone so that they all fitted snugly together. The fit is often so perfect that not even a blade of grass would slide between the stones.

NEW HOME

Bingham did not find great treasure at Machu Picchu, but he did remove more than 46,000 fragments and artifacts, including pottery and stone objects. These were taken back to Yale University, in New Haven, Connecticut. In 2010, just in time for the anniversary celebration of Bingham's discovery of Machu Picchu, Yale agreed to return them. They may not be gold or silver treasure, but they are of great interest to archaeologists. Now they will have a new home in a museum in the old Inca capital, Cuzco.

LEGENDS OF LOST CITIES

Lost cities have fascinated adventurers, explorers, and treasure hunters for centuries. The work of uncovering lost cities, particularly Pompeii, led to the development of the science of archaeology. Today, new sites continue to be discovered, and each one adds to our knowledge of the past.

FACT OR FICTION?

Some lost cities may not exist. The legendary city of Atlantis was first mentioned by the ancient Greek writer Plato, and it has inspired explorers and writers ever since. Over the centuries, there have been many claims for the location of Atlantis, from the Atlantic Ocean to Antarctica. Atlantis may never be found—but then again, people once thought that Troy was only a mythical city!

Stories abound about the City of the Caesars on the southernmost tip of South America. It is said to have been founded by survivors of a Spanish shipwreck. Some legends say it was inhabited by huge giants or by ghosts.

City underwater

Port Royal, on the island of Jamaica, was once
a center for the pirates who raided Spanish treasure
ships. Then, in 1692, a massive earthquake struck. In
one devastating blow, Port Royal and its inhabitants
disappeared beneath the waves! In the 1980s,
underwater archaeologists located the city and
revealed some of its treasures. Several buildings lay
on the seabed almost intact. Archaeologists found
objects such as porcelain cups and bowls, pewter
candlesticks, and silver forks and spoons.

LOOKING FOR LOST CITIES

Today, excavating lost
cities is the work of trained
archaeologists. But the
thrill of finding something
new remains. Do you have
what it takes to search for
lost cities? In addition to
learning about archaeology,
you will need to be fit,
brave, and able to endure
harsh conditions. Most of
all, to make the next great
discovery, you will need
to be lucky!

TIMELINE

c. 2500 BCE
Ubar, in southern Arabia, begins to develop.

c. 700s BCE
The Greek poet Homer writes the *Iliad*.

62 CE
An earthquake devastates large areas of Pompeii, in southern Italy.

79 CE (August 24)
Mount Vesuvius erupts for the first time in 300 years, destroying the city of Pompeii.

c. 300 CE
The city of Ubar collapses into the desert.

c. 1250
Cahokia is one of biggest cities in the world, with a population of up to 20,000. By 1400, it is abandoned.

1438
The Inca Empire develops in South America.

1438–1471
The city of Machu Picchu is possibly constructed now.

1532
Pizarro and his *conquistadors* invade the Inca Empire.

1533
The Spanish execute the Inca king Atahualpa.

1546
The Spanish establish the mining town of Potosi in present-day Peru.

1572
The Spanish execute the last *Sapa Inca* (king) and destroy the Inca settlements of Vitcos and Vilcabamba.

late 1500s
Domenico Fontana rediscovers the city of Pompeii.

1763
A stone with the inscription *Rei publicae Pompeianorum* is uncovered at Pompeii.

1860
Italian archaeologist Giuseppe Fiorelli takes charge of excavations at Pompeii.

1871
Heinrich Schliemann begins excavations to uncover Troy.

1911
American explorer Hiram Bingham is led to the ruins of Machu Picchu.

1912 and 1915
Bingham returns to Peru, partly funded by Yale University.

1931
British explorer Bertram Thomas is the first European to cross the Rub al-Khali.

1945
"Priam's treasure" is taken by Soviet troops to Moscow.

1991–1992
American filmmaker Nicholas Clapp leads an expedition to find Ubar.

1993
"Priam's treasure" is put on display at the Pushkin Museum in Moscow.

2011
Yale University agrees to return artifacts from Machu Picchu to Peru.

GLOSSARY

amateur person who is interested in a subject but does not have a degree or formal training in it

archaeologist scientist who specializes in archaeology

archaeology study of the human past by examining remains and ruins such as burial sites and ancient cities

arrogant having an exaggerated sense of one's own importance

artifact anything made by humans, particularly something from the past

besiege surround with hostile forces

bunker defensive fortification, usually underground

camel caravan long line of camels used to transport goods, often across desert regions

conquistadors Spanish word for the "conquerors" who invaded Central and South America in the 16th century

epic poem long poem that tells a story

frankincense resin, similar to gum, that comes from the trunks of Boswellia trees in southern Arabia

Gold Rush rush of people to an area where gold has been discovered. The most famous event of this type was the California Gold Rush in the 1840s, when gold was discovered in the Rocky Mountains of North America.

indigo dye natural blue dye extracted from plants

inscription words or symbols carved into a stone or other object

Islam worldwide religion that began in Arabia in the 7th century. Followers of Islam are called Muslims. Muslims believe in one God, called Allah.

mortar paste that holds bricks and stones together in a wall

mosaic picture made up of tiny pieces of stone, glass, or other materials. The Romans often decorated their houses with mosaic floors.

nomadic describes a lifestyle in which people move from place to place, rather than settling in one spot

pewter metal made from a mixture of tin with a small amount of another metal, often copper or lead

porcelain type of very fine china

precipice steep and high rock face

pyroclastic flow dense mass of hot ash, lava fragments, and gases ejected explosively from a volcano, usually at great speed

Qur'an holy book of Islam

satellite object that is sent into orbit around Earth by humans

sinkhole hole in the ground formed when the roof of an underground cave collapses

smallpox highly infectious disease caused by a virus. It was unknown in the Americas before the arrival of Europeans in the 15th century.

Soviet from the Soviet Union, or USSR, a Communist state that existed between 1922 and 1991 in what are now Russia and other countries

space shuttle space airplane that flew between Earth and the orbiting International Space Station from 1981 until 2011

FIND OUT MORE

Books

Bingham, Jane. *The Inca Empire* (Time Travel Guides). Chicago: Raintree, 2008.

Bingham, Jane, and Anne Millard. *The Usborne Internet-Linked Encyclopedia of the Ancient World*. Tulsa, Okla.: EDC, 2005.

Colum, Padraic. *The Adventures of Odysseus and the Tale of Troy* (rewritten for children). New York: Macmillan, 2010.

Rubalcaba, Jill, and Eric Cline. *Digging for Troy: From Homer to Hisarlik*. Watertown, Mass.: Charlesbridge, 2011.

van Rose, Susanna. *Volcanoes and Earthquakes* (Eyewitness). New York: Dorling Kindersley, 2008.

Wagner, Heather Lehr. *Pompeii* (Lost Worlds and Mysterious Civilizations). New York: Chelsea House, 2012.

Web sites

dsc.discovery.com/tv/pompeii
Visit this Discovery web site to learn more about the doomed city of Pompeii. This site also includes updates on the most recent discoveries at Pompeii.

video.nationalgeographic.com/video/kids/people-places-kids/ peru-machupicchu-kids
On this National Geographic web site, you can watch a film of Machu Picchu as it is today.

www.saudiaramcoworld.com/issue/198606/the.wabar.meteorite.htm
Philby's discoveries in the Rub al-Khali are explored on this site.

www.saudiaramcoworld.com/issue/198903/crossing.the.rub..htm
This diary account of what it is like to cross the vast Rub al-Khali desert was written by American traveler Eric Mandaville.

Places to visit

The American Museum of Natural History
Central Park West at 79th Street
New York, New York 10024-5192
www.amnh.org
The American Museum of Natural History is home to many of the
world's greatest historical treasures, including some from ancient Rome
and the Americas.

Smithsonian National Museum of Natural History
10th Street and Constitution Avenue, NW
Washington, D.C. 20560
www.mnh.si.edu
The National Museum of Natural History has archaeological finds from many
of the civilizations mentioned in this book, and more.

One of the best places to find out about the Inca civilization is
Machu Picchu or the Incan Museum in Cuzco, Peru.

If you get the chance to travel to Italy, you could also visit the site at Pompeii
and the National Archaeological Museum in Naples, which houses
many of the artifacts taken from Pompeii. If you cannot travel to any of these
places, find them online or look out for exhibitions in museums near you.

Topics for further research

- Find out more about the Cahokia earth mounds—who built them,
  and why (cahokiamounds.org).

- Inspired by Heinrich Schliemann, an amateur archaeologist named
  Arthur Evans excavated the site at Knossos in Greece. Who lived
  at Knossos? What did Evans find?

- El Dorado was a famous lost empire in South America, famed for its gold
  and wealth. In 1541, a *conquistador* named Gonzalo Pizarro plunged into
  the jungle with a group of 300 fellow-soldiers in search of El Dorado.
  See what you can find out about the legend of El Dorado.

INDEX